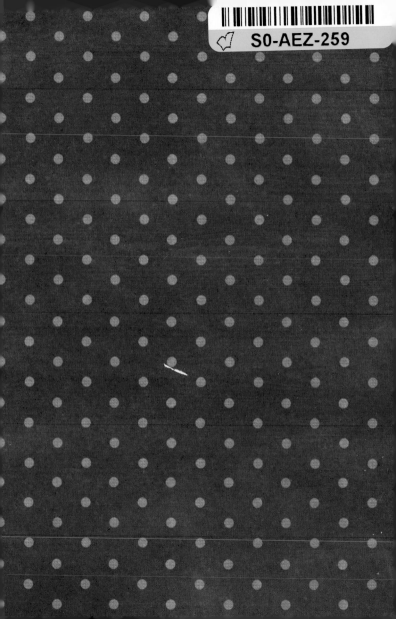

DINNERTIME DEVOTIONS

BITE-SIZED
INSPIRATION
FOR FAMILIES

BroadStreet
PUBLISHING

BroadStreet Publishing Group LLC
Savage, Minnesota, USA
Broadstreetpublishing.com

DINNERTIME DEVOTIONS

© 2018 by BroadStreet Publishing

ISBN 978-1-4245-5583-3 (hardcover)
ISBN 978-1-4245-5672-4 (ebook)

Entries composed by Janelle Breckell, Jason and Rebekah Haché, and Michelle Winger.

Design by Chris Garborg | garborgdesign.com
Edited by Michelle Winger | literallyprecise.com

Printed in China.

18 19 20 21 22 23   7 6 5 4 3 2 1

INTRODUCTION

Celebrate the most connected part of your day with *Dinnertime Devotions*.

This devotional is filled with enlightening Scriptures, meaningful devotions, and conversation starters. As you participate in discussion and activities, take time as a family to write down important goals, prayer requests, praise reports, and memorable moments. And always remember to thank God for his many blessings.

For what we are about to receive, may we be truly thankful.

Only for You

No king is saved by his great army.
No warrior escapes by his great strength.
Horses can't bring victory.
They can't save by their strength.
But the Lord looks after those who fear him.
He watches over those who put their hope in his love.

PSALM 33:16-18 ICB

Not everyone who can sing well will become famous. The fastest runner at your school might not make it to the Olympics. Sometimes we think that to be the best means that the whole world will notice us. But God didn't give us gifts so that we could be famous; he gave us gifts so that we can show the world his love.

God wants you to do your best with the skills that he has given you, but most of all, he wants you to do it with a good heart.

PRAYER:

God, thank you for the gifts you have given us.
Help us to do our best with these gifts.
We trust that you will show us how to use them
for others' good and your glory.

ACTIVITY:

Write down something that the person sitting on your left is really good at. Take a moment as a family to acknowledge each of the strengths that were written down.

vivi - dancing/acting

mum - good at being sweet

Ollie - good at creating

Dad - good at IT stuff and helping people.

Who Cares?

When I suffer, this comforts me:
Your promise gives me life.

PSALM 119:50 ICB

Sometimes life is not fair. Maybe you have been blamed for something that wasn't your fault. Or someone has made fun of you for the way you look. You might have embarrassed yourself playing sports. Perhaps people in your family are fighting and it makes you sad. There are a lot of things that can upset you.

Guess what? Jesus has made a promise to always be with us. He sent the Holy Spirit, our helper, to whisper to us when things go wrong and remind us that we are loved.

PRAYER:

God, when we feel really upset, please let us hear your Holy Spirit reminding us of your great promises. Thank you that you watch over us, and you care about us deeply.

ACTIVITY:

Ask each person around the table if there is anything that is making them sad or upset right now. Take some time to hear each concern and pray for those who need comfort.

African elephants live in herds. Elephant moms get help with their babies and young calves from the very moment they are born. In these caring communities, older elephants show younger elephants how to live and what to eat; they slow down when the young elephants can't walk as quickly, and they help new moms figure out how to take care of their young. There is no lack of comfort and support in the caring elephant world.

Strong and Brave

*"Remember that I commanded you to be strong
and brave. So don't be afraid. The Lord your God
will be with you everywhere you go."*

Joshua 1:9 icb

What does it feel like to stand up in front of a class to read something out loud, or talk to a group of people about a project you just finished? Do you get a little nervous? Do you get *really* nervous? Don't worry, many people are not comfortable talking in front of a large group.

The next time you are facing something that makes you nervous, you can remember that you have a big strong God standing right next to you. He can give you the courage to do anything. Take a deep breath and relax! God is on your side.

PRAYER:

God, please help us to overcome our fears by remembering that you are always with us. Thank you for the courage you give us. We need your strength to help us get through every challenging moment we face.

ACTIVITY:

Have everyone write down one thing they need courage for this week. Remember to pray for each request, and come back to this page later to see how God answered your prayers.

Did you know...

Glossophobia is the fear of public speaking. It is suggested that maybe even as high as 75% of all people are afraid of getting up in front of a group of people to talk. If this is true, it would make glossophobia the world's number one fear!

Fighting for You

In all these things we are more than conquerors through him who loved us.

ROMANS 8:37 NIV

Imagine you are fighting a battle with all your might. There are swords flying and warriors falling. Your eyes are drawn toward your fearless leader slaying dragons right and left. Enemies who dare attack him lose terribly because he has so much power and he is incredibly skilled. That leader is Jesus, and he fights for you!

Jesus fills us with his strength to face everything that comes our way. He is on our side, and nothing can keep us down. Nothing can defeat us. Nothing we are going through is too hard for Jesus to help give us victory over. All we have to do is keep our eyes fixed on him, and ask him for help.

PRAYER:

Jesus, thank you for fighting our battles with us and for us. We want to get into the habit of turning to you each time we need help. We know that you hear us and you see us. Through you, we can be more than conquerors!

ACTIVITY:

Play a few games of thumb wrestling in pairs. Although thumb wrestling isn't a serious battle, it sure is fun to win. Is there someone who seems to win more than others? How would it feel to win every time you played? With Jesus on your side, you can win every battle you face.

Did you know...

The "peace sign" that we commonly make with our fingers, was a sign that Winston Churchill made popular during WWII. It didn't stand for peace, it actually symbolized victory. Churchill's "V for Victory" sign was used frequently by the Allies during the war to show solidarity with each other and defiance against the enemy.

A Safe Cage

When I am afraid, I will put my confidence in you.
Yes, I will trust the promises of God.
And since I am trusting him,
what can mere man do to me?

Have you ever seen a bird in a cage with a cat sitting outside watching the bird? If you haven't seen it in real life, you many have seen it in a number of cartoons or shows. If there were no cage, the bird would be really afraid, but the bird knows that it is safe inside its cage.

We can feel as strong and sure as that little bird in the cage because we have the best protection of all—our Heavenly Father. That cat might be sitting outside the cage waiting to pounce, but we can trust that God is faithful, and he is taking good care of us.

PRAYER:

God, when we are afraid, help us to know that you can erase all our fears. When we feel like bad things are trying to get to us, help us feel safe and secure in your cage of protection, knowing you care for us and you are watching over us.

ACTIVITY:

Put a toy under an upside-down drinking glass on the table. Take a small rubber ball and roll it toward the toy. Do you think the toy needs to be worried about the ball hitting it when the toy is under the glass? Now take the glass away and roll the ball toward the toy. Is it possible to knock the toy over when it's not protected by the glass? How is this like the lesson we read earlier?

Did you know...

Orangutan mothers are very protective of their young. They never put their babies down and often nurse them through the first six or seven years of life. They spend a large amount of time high up in the trees building new nests every day. It would be pretty difficult for a predator to get to that baby orangutan when it's holding onto its mother.

FRUIT SNACKS

LOVE

Brainstorm as many ideas you can
about how you can show love to others.
Circle your favorite three and aim to
complete each of them.

Storing Goodness

You have stored up so many good things.
You have stored them up for those who have respect for you.
You give those things while everyone watches.
You give them to people who run to you for safety.

PSALM 31:19 NIRV

This verse says that God is storing up good things. What exactly are those good things? Safety? Peace? A quiet heart when life is crazy? Joy even when your best friend is mad at you? It would seem that his goodness could be all of these and much more.

God has so much goodness that he actually has to store it. If he didn't, we would be overwhelmed by it all at once! The goodness of God is for those of us who know and love him. God rewards us more than we could imagine in our wildest dreams when we choose to follow and obey him.

PRAYER:

God, we trust in your goodness. Thank you that you store up so many good things for those who love you. We have been so blessed by you and we acknowledge that today.

ACTIVITY:

Pass the book around the table and have each person write down one good thing they are thankful for. Pass the book around again. And one more time. You could probably pass the book around the table ten more times and not run out of things to thank God for. Spend some time thanking him for the good things everyone has listed.

Did you know...

If you look up "good things," you will stumble upon many physical things that people call good: space savers, fancy water, burgers and fries, stain removers, doorstops, garden tools, pillows, the list goes on and on. There are companies, charities, and foundations that all try to define what goodness is either by selling good products or naming their brand with the word good. God has his own definition of the word, and what we call good pales in comparison.

Working with Joy

In all the work you are doing, work the best you can. Work as if you were working for the Lord, not for men. Remember that you will receive your reward from the Lord, which he promised to his people. You are serving the Lord Christ.

Colossians 3:23-24 ICB

Most of us have to work. Students do homework, children do chores, and parents work to take care of their families. Sometimes jobs can be fun, and sometimes they can be boring or stressful! The Bible says to remember that we do our jobs for God, not just for others.

God loves us so much and we are promised a great reward if we work hard. If we can learn to think about our different types of work as jobs given to us by God, we will be surprised how much it helps our attitude toward our work.

PRAYER:

God, we want to serve you. We are excited to receive the reward you have waiting for us. Help us to work with our whole hearts, knowing I'm pleasing you.

ACTIVITY:

Look at the person on your right. Do you know what kind of work they have to do? Take turns asking each other about the jobs each of you do. Then thank each other for your hard work, and be reminded of the reward that is coming.

Did you know...

There's a reason we say "busy as a beaver." Beavers begin preparing their winter homes late in the summer and work hard through the fall to make sure everything is ready. They spend months gathering wood by chipping away at tree trunks with their teeth! That seems like a lot of hard work.

Created for a Purpose

We know that in all things God works for the good of those who love him, who have been called according to his purpose.

ROMANS 8:28 NIV

What do you dream of doing one day? Can you think of a job that you want to have? Maybe you have a list of exciting places you want to visit, or people you would like to meet.

God has a purpose for your life. He wants you to do things you love, and he wants you to do those while you are loving and following him. You might not know what your purpose in life is, but you will find it when you choose to love God with all of your heart.

PRAYER:

God, thank you that you have created us each with things we really enjoy. Help us to find our purpose, as individuals and as a family, in loving and serving you.

ACTIVITY:

Have everyone write down two things they would like to do some day. Choose one person to read the wish list out loud. After each wish is read, see if everyone can guess who wrote it down.

I Am Enough

"Before I formed you in your mother's body I chose you.
Before you were born I set you apart to serve me.
I appointed you to be a prophet to the nations."

JEREMIAH 1:5 NIRV

It's amazing to think that before we were all born, God knew us. Nobody else knew us before we were born, not even our parents. God knew because he planned our lives right from their tiny beginnings.

Most parents are proud of their children, even if they don't say it very often. Mothers and fathers love their children just because the children belong to them. Imagine how much more God loves each one of us. He is so proud of us because we belong to him, and he has great things in store for our lives.

PRAYER:

God, when we feel small or insignificant, help us to know in our hearts that we are yours. You have a special plan for each of us, and we thank you that you created us to serve you. Help us to see how very important we are to you.

ACTIVITY:

Using washable markers, color everyone's thumbprint and stamp it on the page. Take some time to acknowledge the difference you see in the patterns and shapes of each thumbprint.

A Special Song

Your love is better than life.
I will praise you.
I will praise you as long as I live.
I will lift up my hands in prayer to your name.
I will be content as if I had eaten the best foods.
My lips will sing. My mouth will praise you.

PSALM 63:3-5 ICB

What could be better than spending a day at a fun park, eating your favorite food, and laughing with your friends? The writer of Psalm 63 thought that Jesus' love was better than anything he had ever experienced in his life.

Do you think you could agree with the psalmist? God is so good to us, and he has done many amazing things to show us his love. Let's take some time today to praise him for the wonderful life he has given us.

PRAYER:

God, your love is better than anything in this life! Help us to remember your many blessings every day. We want to praise you for your continued faithfulness and goodness to us.

ACTIVITY:

Write a song of praise to God from your family. Have each person help create a line or two that gives glory to God for all he is and all he has done. God delights in our praises. He loves when we take time to create special songs to him from our hearts.

Did you know...

A male songbird can sing about 2,000 songs in one day. If a songbird never slept, he would sing a different song every forty-five seconds. Can you imagine singing that many songs?

FRUIT SNACKS

JOY

Write down the names of everyone at the
table. Next to their name, write down how
they bring joy to the family. Remember to
encourage these qualities in each other.

Love Defined

Love is patient and kind. Love is not jealous, it does not brag,
and it is not proud. Love is not rude, is not selfish, and does
not become angry easily. Love does not remember wrongs
done against it. Love takes no pleasure in evil, but rejoices
over the truth. Love patiently accepts all things.
It always trusts, always hopes, and always continues strong.

1 CORINTHIANS 13:4-7 ICB

You are patient and kind. You are not jealous, you do not brag,
you are not rude or selfish. You don't become angry easily, and you
don't remember when people do wrong things to you. Does that
sound like you? Does it sound like anyone you know?

Love is not just something you feel, but something you choose,
even when you don't want to. It means putting other's needs before
your own just like Jesus did.

PRAYER:

Jesus, you have shown us so much love and patience. Teach
us how to love like you do and help us to put others first.

ACTIVITY:

Take turns going around the table reciting the following statement and filling in the blank: "I feel loved when _____." (For example: I feel loved when daddy makes me breakfast.)

Did you know...

Forrest Lunsway certainly knew about patient love! At the age of 72, he began to pursue a widow named Rose Pollard. She liked spending time with Forrest but kept telling him she had no interest in being his wife. Their friendship continued but Forrest never gave up on the idea of marrying Rose. After 20 years of pursuing her, he proposed! Rose said no, but joked that if he lived to be 100, she would then marry him. So, eight years later, on his 100th birthday, Forrest and Rose were married at last!

Beautifully Different

*God created human beings in his image. In the image of God
he created them. He created them male and female.*

Genesis 1:27 icb

Sometimes we get jealous of the famous actors and rock stars on
the covers of magazines. There are days when we want to be as
good looking or popular as they are.

God did not create us to be like everyone else. He made us special.
What we are good at, others might not be. We shouldn't look at
what other people are good at and feel bad about ourselves. Instead,
we should celebrate how wonderfully different God made us!

PRAYER:

God, thank you for reminding us of how different and
special you created us to be. We are so thankful that you are a
creative God and we can enjoy each other's gifts and talents.

ACTIVITY:

Create a work of art as a family! First, have each person choose a different colored marker or crayon. Then pass this book around the table and have each person add their contribution to the masterpiece. When the artistic juices stop flowing, take turns interpreting your creation.

Did you know...

Some masterpieces take longer to create than others. Mt. Rushmore took 14 years to create, and it took the Egyptians almost 30 years to build some of the pyramids. Amazingly, God created everything in the heavens and the earth in a mere six days. He truly is the greatest creator of all!

Others First

You are still following the ways of the world. Some of you are jealous. Some of you argue. So aren't you following the ways of the world? Aren't you acting like ordinary human beings?

1 Corinthians 3:3 NIRV

Have you ever wanted the toy that your friend got for his or her birthday? Have you been jealous of your brother or sister because they got special time with mom or dad? Do you wish you lived in your neighbor's house, or drove your friend's car?

When we get grumpy about what others have, we are not thinking about their best. We fight because we are only thinking about ourselves. God wants us to be different. He wants us to think about others first, so we are happy when something good happens to them. Can we try to change our attitudes toward other people today?

PRAYER:

God, move our hearts to care for others rather than to only care about what we want. Help us to be genuinely happy for other people when they are blessed with good things.

ACTIVITY:

Have each member of the family share a time when they felt jealous of someone else. How did they act in the moment? Looking back on the situation, would they do or say anything differently?

Did you know...

There are a lot of reasons why God doesn't want us to be jealous. Being jealous for a long time can weaken your immune system, which means you can get sick easier because your body isn't producing enough disease-fighting antibodies!

You Are Rich!

Tell them to use their money to do good. They should be rich in good works and generous to those in need, always being ready to share with others. By doing this they will be storing up their treasure as a good foundation for the future so that they may experience true life.

1 TIMOTHY 6:18-19 NLT

It's hard to save up money. You might be too young to work, so you need your parents to pay for things until you get a few dollars. Or maybe family expenses are high right now and there's not a lot of extra cash to get things you would really like. Money is not the only way we can be rich.

If you don't have a lot of money, but you have a lot of extra time, you can use your time to bless others. What do you do during your free time? Do you watch movies or play games? What ways could you be showing God's love to other people? You can be rich in God's love and choose to share this any time!

PRAYER:

Father, thank you for giving us a lot of love. We want to share that love with those in need. Help us to understand that even if we don't have a lot of money, we are rich because you have blessed us with each other.

34

ACTIVITY:

Go around the table and have each person describe one way that they will share their time or possessions this week.

Listen

"The seed on good soil stands for those with an honest and good heart. Those people hear the message. They keep it in their hearts. They remain faithful and produce a good crop."

LUKE 8:15 NIRV

When you plant a seed, you push it deeply into the soil. A seed won't grow if it is put on a rock because there is nothing for it to dig its roots into.

Sometimes we hear things from God, but we don't really listen. This is like being a seed that gets put on a rock. What we hear can be forgotten and we don't let our life change. When we hear God's words, we need to remember them. Write them down, memorize them. That way, we will be able to understand more about God.

PRAYER:

Lord, thank you that you speak to us. Thank you for your words of truth that we find in the Bible. Help us to remember your words so we can understand more about you.

ACTIVITY:

Write this week's verse on a piece of paper and tape it to your bathroom mirror. Make a point to read it out loud several times this week. Before you know it, God's truth will be planted deep in your heart.

Did you know...

Bats—the only flying mammal—navigate and hunt their prey by emitting high-frequency sounds and using their funnel-shaped ears to listen for the echoes those sounds make as they bounce off nearby objects. By using this "echolocation," they can pinpoint tiny insects in complete darkness. As bats fly through the air, they emit sounds. Based on the frequency and intensity of the returning echoes, they can tell how far away objects are.

PEACE

Write a list of things that make you feel
peaceful. Spend some time quietly reflecting
on these things now.

Speaking Truth

*It is better to correct someone openly
than to love him and not show it.
The slap of a friend can be trusted to help you.
But the kisses of an enemy are nothing but lies.*

PROVERBS 27:5-6 ICB

It is always better to tell the truth. It might be easier to lie sometimes, but it never feels good on the inside. Even though it is hard to tell the truth, you feel a lot better when you do. When you are truthful, people can trust you.

The next time you want to tell a lie, remember that it will only make you feel worse. Speaking the truth is the best way. It keeps you and others from getting hurt. God loves truth, and he loves you!

PRAYER:

God, help us to be brave enough to always tell the truth. Thank you for forgiving us and loving us even when we make mistakes. We want people to be able to trust us, so help us to tell the truth even when it is difficult.

ACTIVITY:

Most of us remember Aesop's Fable about the boy who cried wolf. The boy lied to the villagers three times telling them that a wolf was coming for their sheep. Eventually a real wolf approached, but when the boy cried for help no one came because they thought he was just trying to trick them again. Assign roles to each family member and have fun acting out this story.

A Happy Yes

*Restore to me the joy of your salvation,
and make me willing to obey you.*

PSALM 51:12 NLT

Do you remember a time when you didn't want to do what your parents asked you to do? Maybe they told you to go upstairs and brush your teeth and you chose to ignore them because you didn't want to go to bed. Maybe a teacher or a boss asked you to complete a task you didn't really want to do, so you pretended to forget about it. We have a lot of choices to obey every single day whether we are young or old.

You probably know that in the end it feels really good to do the right thing! Your choices affect other people. When you obey, it makes people happy, and it usually makes you feel happy too. God loves it when we are joyful about obeying him too.

PRAYER:

God, your way is the best way. Help us to choose to obey you and to be joyful about obeying others you have put in our lives as leaders. We trust you with our lives.

ACTIVITY:

Play a few rounds of "Mother May I?" Everyone line up at one end of the room with the designated Mother standing at the opposite end with her back to the group. Each person in the group takes a turn asking, "Mother, may I take (insert #) steps forward." The Mother can choose to grant or deny each request. The first person to reach the Mother takes his or her place and then the group returns to their starting positions and a new round begins.

Did you know...

Little puppies might not seem very obedient, always wanting to play and jump on you. But with positive training they can learn to obey quickly! Most dogs can learn more than 1000 words. Some common tricks dogs learn are to sit, bow, shake, walk backwards, dance, roll over, and play dead.

Blind Trust

You love him even though you have never seen him; though not seeing him, you trust him; and even now you are happy with the inexpressible joy that comes from heaven itself. And your further reward for trusting him will be the salvation of your souls.

1 Peter 1:8-9 TLB

It can be difficult to believe in God because we cannot see him. We like having our friends and family close because they give us hugs, and we can see their faces when we talk to them.

When God created Adam and Eve, they could walk with him in the Garden of Eden. Now because of sin, we can no longer look at God's face directly, but he still walks with us. God is close to us even when we don't know that he is. This is why we can love and trust him even though we cannot see him.

PRAYER:

God, we know you are real even though we cannot see you with our eyes. Thank you for always being with us. Help us to listen to you as you lead us through the obstacles in our lives.

ACTIVITY:

Set up a few obstacles in your living room and then blindfold one family member. Designate someone else to be their guide. Using only their ears to listen to the guide, see which one of you can get from one end of the room to the other with the least amount of bumps!

Jesus tells us in the Bible that if we have faith the size of a mustard seed we can do some pretty amazing things. Mustard seeds are incredibly small measuring only one to two millimeters in diameter, which is about the size of the tip of a pencil. However, some mustard plants can grow up to nine feet tall. It is the third most used spice after salt and pepper and has been around a very long time. Some seeds were found in a Chinese jar that is thought to be 5000 years old!

Good Friends

A real friend sticks closer than a brother.

PROVERBS 18:24 NLT

Sometimes all we want is to be with a good friend and talk or play. We want to share our joys and our worries with someone who really cares. We want to enjoy just hanging out. Everyone needs a friend like that.

Just like you need a good friend, so do other people. Are you being a good friend? God wants you to stick close to your good friends, to care for them and to defend them. God made friendship for our good. Let's be grateful for our friends today.

PRAYER:

God, we are so thankful for good friendships.
Bless all the people in our lives who we call friends today.
Help us to be good friends in return.

ACTIVITY:

Take turns sharing about a time that someone was a good friend to you. How did it make you feel? Discuss ideas about how you can be a good friend to those around you this week.

Did you know...

Some animals have friends that don't look anything like them! Chimpanzees, elephants, baboons, horses, hyenas, dolphins, and bats have all been known to choose BFFs from other species. Maybe it's not always true that "birds of a feather flock together."

Wasted Worry

"Don't worry. Don't say, 'What will we eat?' Or, 'What will we drink?' Or, 'What will we wear?' People who are ungodly run after all those things. Your Father who is in heaven knows that you need them. But put God's kingdom first. Do what he wants you to do. Then all those things will also be given to you."

Matthew 6:31-33 nirv

If you play board games, you will know that there is a start and a finish to every game. As you play a game, there are things that get in the way of you finishing, like not answering a question right, or having to skip a turn.

What if you spent the whole game worrying about what could go wrong? It wouldn't be a very enjoyable game for you. God says that life is like that. You can't keep worrying about what might go wrong. To enjoy life, you need to trust God and look to the finish line—one day you will get to that treasure!

PRAYER:

Jesus, help us keep our eyes and hearts centered on you. We don't want to worry about all the things that could happen to us or to others. There are so many things we cannot control. Help us to be ok with that because we trust in you.

ACTIVITY:

What is your favorite game
to play as a family? Take
thirty minutes to play it
together tonight.

FRUIT SNACKS

PATIENCE

Make a list of things that test your patience.
Now write down a possible solution for each
that will enable you to keep your cool when
these things happen.

Fighting by Your Side

The LORD is faithful;
he will strengthen you and guard you from the evil one.

2 THESSALONIANS 3:3 NLT

Faithful friends stand up for you. A faithful dog sticks close to your side. God is more faithful than either of these! He will never leave you. Even if you feel like you are in the middle of a battle, he will be right there fighting with you.

If people are saying unkind or untrue things about you, God will remind you of what he loves about you. If you feel like nobody cares, God will remind you that he does. He will always help you find joy and peace in your life if you take the time to ask him.

PRAYER:

God, we feel much stronger knowing that you are near. Help us to sense your peace and joy when we feel like we are in the middle of a battle and also when things are going well. You are with us all the time and we are so thankful to you for that.

ACTIVITY:

Have each family member draw a picture of themselves in the middle of a battle, be sure to include God fighting with you. When you're done, take turns explaining what you drew.

Did you know...

Beavers are known for their hard work but they are also very faithful partners. These loyal, flat-tailed friends mate for life, which is on average about ten years. It's no wonder they have to work so hard since they can have up to four babies at a time, who are called kits. Thankfully they share responsibilities when it comes to raising kits, which momma beavers must greatly appreciate.

The Gift of Joy

*"I loved you as the Father loved me. Now remain in my love I
have obeyed my Father's commands, and I remain in his love.
In the same way, if you obey my commands, you will remain
in my love. I have told you these things so that you can have
the same joy I have. I want your joy to be the fullest joy."*

JOHN 15:9-11 ICB

Joy comes into our lives when we follow God's directions. He
rewards us with a whole lot of love. As we stay in this love, we
become full of joy that can be shared with the people around us.

Can you think of anyone that needs more joy in their life? Most
people have busy schedules these days and it seems that this
busyness causes a lot of stress. Maybe you can help people who
seem tense by being a happy person yourself. Happy people are
pleasant to be around, and this is a good representation of Jesus.

PRAYER:

Thank you, God, for your love that gives us so much joy.
Help us to share our joy with those around us. Help us to be
happy people that others enjoy being with.

ACTIVITY:

Some people use the following acronym to help remind them how to experience true joy: Jesus, Others, Yourself. Take a few moments to memorize this as a family. Then have everyone share practical ways they can put Jesus and others before themselves.

Did you know...

Smiles are contagious they say, and it's true! We naturally smile when smiled at. We even have a hard time creating a frown in response to someone who is smiling at us. It's not just our facial muscles that are affected, smiling instantly lifts our mood. God created our bodies to release endorphins that make us happy when we smile or laugh. Maybe laughter really is the best medicine.

Your Thought Life

Letting your sinful nature control your mind leads to death.
But letting the Spirit control your mind leads to life and peace.

ROMANS 8:6 NLT

We drive cars using a steering wheel. The steering wheel controls which way the car goes. When you pull to the right, the car moves right, and when you steer to the left, the car moves left. Did you know you can control your mind like this? You can decide what to think!

The thoughts in our minds are very powerful. The actions we take come from the thoughts we think, so good thoughts lead to good actions. And bad thoughts lead to bad actions. We should be careful what we think about, and make our thoughts would honor God.

PRAYER:

Father God, please fill us with more of your Holy Spirit today so we can control our minds and choose right thoughts that lead to good actions. We want our minds and hearts to be at peace.

ACTIVITY:

As a family, create a list of
actions and what thoughts might
have led to them. (For example:
"I'm hungry" leads to eating
an apple; "He's mean" causes
you to hit your brother;
"I love Mom" makes you give
your mom a hug.) If we want to
act the right way, what thoughts
should we be thinking?

Did you know...

*Mahatma Gandhi didn't
like the way that Britain
was treating India so he
decided to do something
about it. Did he create
an army and start a
war? Did he try to force
Britain out of India?
No, Gandhi decided to
stop eating. That's right,
he stopped eating, and
people started listening.
Through this amazing
example of self-control,
Gandhi was able to
improve the lives of
countless Indians.*

Forgive and Forget

*I will forgive their wickedness
and will remember their sins no more.*

HEBREWS 8:12 NIV

It is so hard to forget the mean things people do to us. We tend to hold on to the hurt and the pain, but that's not what God does. He has a loving heart that forgives. When we say sorry, he makes us clean, as if we did nothing wrong to begin with. He doesn't keep a list of our mistakes. It's like they just disappear.

God doesn't remember our sin, so we don't have to feel guilty or punish ourselves once we've asked for forgiveness either. Isn't this a fantastic promise?

PRAYER:

God, thank you for forgiving us of all the wrong things that we do. Not only do you forgive us, but you don't keep bringing up our faults and sins when we come to you. You forgive and forget. Help us to be more like that with ourselves and with others.

ACTIVITY:

Do we keep a list of the way people sin against us? Have each family member use a pencil to write down a time when someone did something that hurt their feelings. Then pray that God forgives each person responsible for the situation on the list, and after you address each situation, erase it from the list. When you are done crumple up the paper and throw it in the garbage. God doesn't keep lists and neither should we!

Louis Zamperini was one of many brave soldiers who was captured by the enemy in World War II. He was starved and tortured for two years by the people he saw as his enemies. Eventually Louis was released, and do you know what he did? He forgave the men who treated him so horribly. He realized that if Jesus could forgive him, then he had to forgive others. Louis decided to return to the place where he was imprisoned and by the power of Jesus' love, he was able to embrace the very men who had tortured him.

The Body

Each of us has one body with many parts. And the parts do not all have the same purpose. So also we are many persons. But in Christ we are one body. And each part of the body belongs to all the other parts.

ROMANS 12:4-5 NIRV

Can your eyes listen to sounds? Can your ears talk? Can you walk on your nose? No! Your body is made up of different parts, and each part of the body does something special to help you move, grow, and live.

Jesus says that God's family is like a body. We are all different parts and he doesn't want us to be exactly like each other. The best way to make God's family work, is for you to just be you. Everyone needs you to do your special part.

PRAYER:

Father, thank you that you have made each of us different. Help us to remember how important it is to just be ourselves. We want to be who you created us each to be so that we are more effective when we work together.

ACTIVITY:

Complete a puzzle together as a family. Discuss how each piece fits perfectly with each other and if even one piece were missing, the puzzle wouldn't be complete!

FRUIT SNACKS

KINDNESS

Write the letters K-I-N-D-N-E-S-S on this page vertically. Now come up with a way to show kindness beginning with each letter.

Gift of Peace

"I am leaving you with a gift—peace of mind and heart.
And the peace I give is a gift the world cannot give.
So don't be troubled or afraid."

JOHN 14:27 NLT

Everybody likes to get presents! Can you think of a time when you got a gift that you really, really wanted? Or something that you had never be given before?

Jesus describes peace as a gift like this. It's something that only he can give. It's not something that anyone in this world could wrap up for you. It's one of the best gifts because peace helps us to be calm when things are tough. Open up his gift of peace today.

PRAYER:

Jesus, thank you for giving us the gift of peace. When things get hard, help us to remember that we don't have to be afraid because you are with us.

ACTIVITY:

Have each member of the family share about the most exciting gift they have ever received. What made it so special? The person who gave them this gift must have thought they were pretty special. Imagine what God must think of us to give us such amazing gifts!

Did you know...

The United States received a pretty big gift from France over 100 years ago. The Statue of Liberty was built in France and then all 350 individual pieces were shipped across the ocean to be put back together again. She stands 305 feet tall on Liberty Island in New York. If you visited the Statue of Liberty today, you would have to climb 354 steps to reach her crown!

Rich Rewards

Do not throw away your confidence; it will be richly rewarded.
You need to persevere so that when you have done the will of
God, you will receive what he has promised.

HEBREWS 10:35-36 NIV

Hiking is a really long walk through nature. When you go for a hike, you are usually walking up and down hills or mountains. You can get tired and sore and sometimes slip a few times. You might even have to walk through mud.

Have you heard of the word *perseverance?* That would be what it takes to walk up a mountain. You have to work hard to get to the top, but it is beautiful when you get there. God will reward you for a life that you live for him.

PRAYER:

God, help us to keep living life with you.
We know you will reward us for our perseverance
when we finally get to the top of the mountain.

ACTIVITY:

Using a deck of cards, make the biggest, tallest house that you can. Have each person take a turn adding to the structure. If it falls, start over and see if you can make it even bigger. You'll soon discover that perseverance can bring about great results.

It takes a lot of hard work to be successful. In most cases there is lots and lots of failure! Colonel Sanders, founder of the delicious KFC restaurants, brought his famous recipe to over 1,000 places before someone bought it. Thomas Edison failed almost 10,000 times before he successfully invented the electric light. Thankfully, these men learned the importance of perseverance; otherwise today we'd be eating bland chicken by candlelight.

Strong and Sure

You have been my hope, Sovereign Lord,
my confidence since my youth.

Psalm 71:5 niv

There are very few people who have the natural gift of confidence. Most of us struggle with different areas of our lives, often believing that everyone else is probably better at everything than we are.

The only way we can feel truly confident is if we can grasp hold of what God thinks about us. When we know that his ways are perfect, his plans for us are good, and his promises are true, that's when we become bold and secure.

PRAYER:

God, thank you for your promises that are good and true and right. We can be confident in your love for us. Help us to show others where they can find their confidence too.

ACTIVITY:

We can be confident because of the many promises that God makes to us in the Bible. Make a list of all the promises of God that you can think of and post it on the fridge. For the next week whenever you open the fridge, read one of the promises out loud to increase your confidence.

It takes a great deal of confidence to become the President of the United States, and perhaps no one is a better example of this than Abraham Lincoln. Before he became the man you see on the five dollar bill, Abe had lost eight elections, had two businesses fail miserably, and even experienced a nervous breakdown! However, he remained confident in the face of such difficulty and eventually succeeded in becoming the President of the United States.

Not Just Mr. Fix It

*Enter his gates with thanksgiving
and his courts with praise;
give thanks to him and praise his name.*

<small>PSALM 100:4 NIV</small>

How do you ask God for things? Do you complain about what you don't have, or tell him exactly what you want? Sometimes we think of God as our magic guy in the sky who will pay for everything, fix everything, and make sure we have exactly what we want.

God wants us to tell him what we need, what we are afraid of, and how we need help, but he also wants us to tell him when we are happy, thankful, or amazed. He deserves our thanks, so let's tell him how grateful we are today.

PRAYER:

God, thank you for everything good and right you have blessed us with. Help us to focus more on what we are grateful for, and less on what we don't have. We want to reflect gratitude and contentment in our daily lives and learn to choose thankfulness each day.

ACTIVITY:

Make a thankful tree! Draw a simple picture of a tree and have each member of the family write something they are thankful for on each of the branches.

Did you know...

Choosing a lifestyle of gratitude helps you sleep better, boosts your immune system, and increases your levels of optimism. This means you will have a much better outlook on life as you wake up each morning. And you will feel healthier as well!

Quiet Beauty

Your beauty should come from within you—
the beauty of a gentle and quiet spirit that will
never be destroyed and is very precious to God.

1 PETER 3:4 NCV

God sees what is inside our hearts more than what we see in the mirror. Some people are pretty on the outside but not very attractive on the inside. Others are gentle and quiet inside—and *that* is seen as beautiful in the kingdom of heaven.

The more time we spend with Jesus, the more we will reflect his character. Jesus makes us attractive on the inside. He helps us to be kind and loving toward others as we go through our day, and that draws people right back to him.

PRAYER:

Jesus, let your beauty shine through us. Let us reflect the gentle and quiet beauty inside that is so important to you. Thank you for your kindness and compassion toward us. Help us to show the same love to others.

ACTIVITY:

Pass a hand mirror around the table. Take turns sharing both inner and outer beauty traits of the person who is holding the mirror.

Did you know...

Standards of beauty change over time and according to location. In some places of the world, white skin, crooked teeth, and facial tattoos are considered beautiful. The ideal thinness portrayed in the western world today is achievable by less than 5% of the female population. In other cultures, it is much more attractive for women to carry extra weight. Maybe it's time to stop focusing on our outward appearance, and start spending time on beautifying our hearts. Beautiful people on the inside are attractive in every culture!

FRUIT SNACKS

GOODNESS

Write down definitions of what you think the word *good* means. Thank God for all the good things he has given you, and for being the very definition of the word.

Get Wise

Getting wisdom is the wisest thing you can do!
And whatever else you do, develop good judgment.

PROVERBS 4:7 NLT

If you couldn't find a trash can, would you throw your garbage on the ground? If you didn't know the answer to a question at school, would you look at someone else's answer? If you saw someone drop their money, would you pick it up and keep it?

We have to make decisions so many times in one day! The Bible says that we need to get wisdom. When we ask for wisdom, we choose to do the right thing. And we usually know what that is because we know what Jesus would do.

PRAYER:

Father God, help us to make good decisions and to be wise in all that we do. Teach us to consider whether what we're thinking about doing is a good or bad idea. We want to act with wisdom, so we trust that you will give that to us.

ACTIVITY:

Good idea or bad idea? Read aloud the following list, asking your family to shout out, "Good idea!" or "Bad idea!" Feel free to add to the list.

+ Make fun of the new kid at school.

+ Clean up your room the first time you are asked.

+ Take money from mom or dad's wallet without asking.

+ Ignore your friend when they are sad because you don't feel like listening to their problems.

+ Volunteer at a fundraiser that will help a family in need.

+ Invite a friend to go to church with you.

+ Get revenge on someone who was mean to you.

Quick Fix

Let's not get tired of doing what is good. At just the right time we will reap a harvest of blessing if we don't give up.

GALATIANS 6:9 NLT

When you plant a seed in a pot and wait for it to grow, it can take a very long time for a little sprout to show. Wouldn't it take even longer to see flowers on the plant?

God says that sometimes the results of our good works can take time to start showing, just like that seed being planted in a pot. We need to have patience and keep doing good. At the right time, God will show us the good that has come from doing the right thing.

PRAYER:

Father, we want to follow you and be good examples. Help us to be patient while we wait for the results of our good works to show.

ACTIVITY:

Setup a balloon relay. Divide into two teams. Each player must walk from one end of the room and back to their team while balancing a balloon on a spoon. If the balloon falls, the player must go back to the beginning and start over. You will soon find that patience pays off in the end.

Did you know...

Today it takes builders only a few months to construct an average home. It took the Egyptians over twenty years to build the Pyramid in Giza! This colossal structure contains over two million stones. It's believed to have had over 100,000 people working together to get the huge pyramid built, and it still stands today. Those people had to wait a very long time to see their work completed.

Showing Kindness

"Is there anyone still left in Saul's family? I want to show kindness to this person for Jonathan's sake!"

2 SAMUEL 9:1 ICB

When you meet your friend's brother or sister, father or mother, you know that you should be polite and nice because you want to do the right thing for your friend.

King David did this in the Bible. He loved his friend Jonathan so much that he asked if there was anyone else that he could be kind to because he wanted to honor his friend. What would happen if we asked that question each day? Is there anyone we can show kindness to today?

PRAYER:

God, remind us to ask who we can show kindness to each day. Help us to listen to your voice and to be great friends to others. There are so many ways we can bless those around us. Give us ideas for how we can best show kindness to others.

ACTIVITY:

As a family, brainstorm ways
that each of you can be kind
to a friend this week. Or,
pick something you can do as
a family to bless someone in
your neighborhood this week.
Simple things like raking leaves,
shoveling a driveway, or taking a
plate of cookies to your neighbor
can be a big blessing.

Did you know...

*Perhaps no human being
embodied kindness more
than Mother Teresa.
She spent her life caring
for the sick and the
homeless: the people that
society wished to forget.
Even after her own
death, Mother Teresa's
kindness still has a global
impact through the
organization she started
named The Sisters of the
Missionaries of Charity.
This charity continues
to care for people in 123
countries around the
world.*

What Is Considerate?

"I give you a new command. Love one another. You must love one another, just as I have loved you. If you love one another, everyone will know you are my disciples."

JOHN 13:34-35 NIRV

How do you know when people are considerate? They smile, share their things, and speak with kindness. Considerate people make us feel good. They are great to be around. They seem to have a lot of friends.

Jesus said that we can show his love by loving one another. People will know that there is something wonderful about us (and about Jesus) just by watching how we treat other people! Isn't that great? We don't have to say anything; Jesus just asks us to be considerate of each other.

PRAYER:

God, open our eyes to see where we can be examples of your love and kindness today. Let others see you in us as we choose to be considerate in everything we say and do.

ACTIVITY:

Put it into practice! Role play different situations like ordering food at a restaurant, receiving a gift from a grandparent, comforting a friend who falls down, etc. Describe the situation and give your child a role to play. Encourage them to use their best manners and show consideration in each situation.

Still My Thoughts

When you are angry, do not sin. And do not go on being angry all day. Do not give the devil a way to defeat you.

EPHESIANS 4:26-27 ICB

When was the last time you felt so angry that you wanted to kick something or throw things around the room? It's pretty normal to feel angry about things, but you have to be careful about what you do with that anger.

What would happen if you hurt yourself, or someone else, or damaged something while you were angry? It would make the situation worse, right? That's why God's way says to find a way to calm down so that you don't keep thinking about your anger. Ask Jesus to help you settle down, and then do something else—like read a book, write a letter, or kick a ball around!

PRAYER:

Father God, help us to let go of our anger. Give us ways to do something right when we are angry instead of doing something that we will regret. Thank you for your grace and self-control that is available when we ask you for it. You are such a kind and forgiving God.

ACTIVITY:

Take turns sharing a time when you felt really angry. How did you handle the situation? Would you do anything differently next time you feel angry? Brainstorm some healthy responses to conflict that you can try another time.

Rocks Don't Change

Trust in the Lord forever,
for the Lord, the Lord himself, is the Rock eternal.

Isaiah 26:4 niv

When people talk about the person they trust the most, they might describe that person as being their rock. A rock put in a box for many years will look exactly the same on the day the box is re-opened. Rocks don't change.

The same goes for God. He does not change. He is always present, always caring, always delighted to spend time with us. If we choose to pray every day, or we only remember to pray at church, he doesn't ignore us. He listens every time. We can always count on God to be faithful and good.

PRAYER:

God, you are our rock. We can trust you with our lives because we know you will never take back your promises, and you are always good. You are steady and unchanging. Thank you that we can cling to you when everything else is changing around us.

ACTIVITY:

It's time to get out those old family photo albums. Show your children pictures of when you were young and when they were babies. After discussing how much everyone has changed over the years, recognize that God never changes; he is the same yesterday, today, and forever.

FRUIT SNACKS

GENTLENESS

Make a list of things that you need to be
gentle with. Now write next to each thing
how you can show gentleness.

Shiny and New

*Anyone who belongs to Christ has become a new person.
The old life is gone; a new life has begun!*

2 CORINTHIANS 5:17 NLT

Have you ever seen a very dirty car go through a car wash and come out sparkling clean? When we accept Jesus into our hearts, he forgets all the bad, ugly things we have done, and he makes us shiny and new—like that nice clean car.

We all have bad things we would like to forget, like mean words we've said and people we've hurt. Every day, we can tell Jesus we are sorry for our sin and he washes that yucky dirt away.

PRAYER:

Jesus, I'm so happy that you can take our sin away. Thank you for forgiving us and washing away our dirt so we can be clean. Help us to come to you as soon as we have sinned and ask for forgiveness, so we don't stay dirty for long.

ACTIVITY:

Do the dishes as a family tonight. Find a way for everyone to get involved with either washing or drying. Talk about how no matter how many times the dishes get dirty, they can always be washed clean. Jesus is faithful to forgive us no matter how many times we mess up.

Did you know...

People have been using soap for over 2,000 years. Groups like the Celts and Phoenicians were both known to make soap by boiling animal fats and mixing it with ashes from a wood fire. They didn't use it to wash their bodies, but rather to cure animal skins or clean their clothes. It was the Romans who first started using soap to wash their bodies. Their idea stuck! Today over ten billion pounds of soap is produced. One third of that is created and consumed in the United States alone.

Laid Low

Give me life, as you have promised.

PSALM 119:25 ICB

Even people in the Bible felt sad sometimes. It's okay to feel upset, and it's okay to say that you are sad. Maybe a friend has been unkind to you, or your parents, teacher, or boss yelled at you, or you were left out of a game. Maybe you didn't play well at your sports practice this week.

Don't give up! God knows when you are upset and he cares when you feel bad. When you are discouraged, it's time to ask God to speak to you. Do you know what he will say? He will say that he loves you, and he will encourage you to carry on.

PRAYER:

Dear God, in those times when we are most upset, help us to ask you for your words of truth. Thank you that you will encourage us with your love and comfort when we are sad.

ACTIVITY:

Take turns speaking an encouraging word to the person on your right. Try to be creative and lean on God's promises in the Bible for ideas. For example, "God will renew your strength" (Isaiah 40:31). "God is always with you" (Joshua 1:9).

Did you know...

Geese fly in a "V" formation to help break the wind resistance, making it easier for the group to fly. They take turns being in the front and back, giving each a break from the hard work of leading the pack. Geese will honk to encourage one another onward, and if a goose gets hurt or sick, other geese will not leave its side until it heals.

Rock Solid

"The rain came down, the streams rose, and the winds blew and beat against that house; yet it did not fall, because it had its foundation on the rock."

MATTHEW 7:25 NIV

Sometimes life is like a huge storm. It beats you down, tosses you around, and carries you away in a flood of troubles and worries. It seems like bad stuff happens all at once. When bad things happen, who do you run to?

The Bible says that the best way to make sure you can stand tall in a storm is to know about God and to have faith in his promises. Then you will be like a house that has a strong foundation, and will not fall apart in a storm.

PRAYER:

God, we know that no matter what we face, we will not fall if you are with us. We choose to believe this today, and we say together, "We trust in you for protection."

ACTIVITY:

Memorize this verse as a family tonight, "Lord, my God, I trust in you for protection. Save me and rescue me from those who are chasing me" (Psalm 7:1, NCV). Come up with actions to help you memorize the text. Say it with the actions at least seven times together. Test each other throughout the week by calling out, "Security check!" Whenever someone says this, whoever is in the room needs to stop and recite the verse with the motions.

Did you know...

Storms can have devastating effects especially when people are caught off guard. We often hear about hurricanes and tornados, but did you know that ice storms can be just as destructive? One such storm hit New England and southeast Canada in January of 1998, which caused collective damage totaling 4.4 billion dollars. The three-inch ice accumulation was responsible for downing millions of trees and left 500,000 residents of New England without power for days.

Don't Panic

"Don't worry, because I am with you.
Don't be afraid, because I am your God.
I will make you strong and will help you.
I will support you with my right hand that saves you."

ISAIAH 41:10 ICB

Is there something you are worried about, making it hard for you to feel okay about things? God tells us we don't need to be afraid. He will strengthen us and help us. He holds us in his hands.

Think of a steep path that goes around and up a huge cliff. Imagine yourself walking on it. You might think that you could fall. Picture God standing right next to you, holding you up. He's not going to let you fall, and he'll give you strength to take another step. It's his promise to you!

PRAYER:

God, we don't have to be afraid because you are holding us, keeping us safe when life throws things our way. Thank you for being near to us.

ACTIVITY:

Practice trust falls tonight! Have each child take turns closing their eyes and falling backwards into the arms of a parent. Remind each other that even when we feel like we're falling, God is always there to catch us.

Faithful without Fail

Let us hold firmly to the hope that we have confessed.
We can trust God to do what he promised.

HEBREWS 10:23 ICB

It can be disappointing when we have plans and then for some reason they don't happen. Maybe your friend couldn't come over because they got sick, or your family was planning to go to the beach and it started to rain. Sometimes people just don't show up when they said they would!

God is not like this at all. The Bible says that he is faithful. This means that he always, always, always does what he has promised. He is committed to us. We can trust him to do what he says he will do.

PRAYER:

God, we pray that we will always remember you and the promises you have made. Thank you that you are committed to us. You want what is the very best for us. All of our hope is in you, and we know you won't disappoint us.

ACTIVITY:

All throughout Scripture, God's people were commanded to create physical reminders of his faithfulness. Create your own physical reminder of God's commitment to your family. It could be as simple as decorating a piece of paper with the word "Faithful" on it, and hanging it on your fridge. Be creative, and make sure you place your creation in a prominent place for everyone to see throughout the week.

Did you know...

How long have your parents been married? Five, ten, twenty, maybe thirty years? Well I bet it's not as long as Herbert and Zelmyra Fisher. They have been married for a whopping 86 years and hold the Guinness World Record for longest marriage! People often ask them what the secret is to a long lasting marriage and Zelmyra confidently replies, "There isn't any secret. It was only God that kept us together."

The Best Outfit

You are God's chosen people. You are holy and dearly loved.
So put on tender mercy and kindness as if they were your
clothes. Don't be proud. Be gentle and patient.

COLOSSIANS 3:12 NIRV

What is your favorite thing to wear? Is it a certain pair of jeans, sweatpants, or a sports shirt? Maybe you enjoy dressing up in a costume, or perhaps you just like wearing your pajamas!

The Bible talks about putting on clothes of kindness, gentleness, and patience. What would that look like? Wearing those clothes would mean that we would make decisions to be kind, gentle, loving people all day long. When we remember to treat others with kindness and mercy, we will always feel like we are wearing our best clothes.

PRAYER:

Father God, help us to remember to dress properly each day, putting on good things like kindness, patience, mercy, and gentleness, so we are ready to share your love with everyone we encounter.

ACTIVITY:

Gather up some paper and crayons! Have everyone draw a picture of themselves showing gentleness and kindness toward someone. When everyone is finished drawing, go around the table letting each person share what they drew.

Did you know...

Gorillas may look fierce but they are really quite gentle. These shy vegetarians can weigh up to 430 pounds, which is quite surprising since their diet consists mostly of fruit, leaves, and seeds. They are a constant reminder that you can't always judge the heart by the outward appearance.

FRUIT SNACKS

FAITHFULNESS

Make a list of the ways God has been faithful
to your family. Spend time thanking him
together for his faithfulness to you.

Working Together

There is neither Jew nor Gentile, neither slave nor free, nor is there male and female, for you are all one in Christ Jesus.

GALATIANS 3:28 NIV

Do you ever have to divide a group of people into smaller groups? There are sometimes hard choices to make about which side we are going to be on. It can be really difficult to choose sides.

The Bible says that we are all part of God's big family. We need to make sure we include everyone who is in this group. God doesn't want us to be separated; he wants us all to be together!

PRAYER:

Jesus, help us to see your people as part of one big family. We want to all get along and love each other well, so we can please you and show others that your family is something everyone should want to be a part of.

ACTIVITY:

Play the unity game. Link arms with each other and form a circle. Try moving throughout the house without letting go. You will discover that unity works better when people communicate and help each other.

Coming Soon

Always be full of joy in the Lord; I say it again, rejoice! Let everyone see that you are unselfish and considerate in all you do. Remember that the Lord is coming soon. Don't worry about anything; instead, pray about everything; tell God your needs, and don't forget to thank him for his answers.

PHILIPPIANS 4:4-6 TLB

Do you like when you have friends or relatives coming over to your house? It's exciting as you prepare for them to arrive. You might clean, or start getting the food ready. You might set up a game to play.

We have a promise that Jesus will come back one day. That should fill us with happiness and excitement! While you are waiting, remember there are things to do. Be kind to people. Show the love of God to others. Pray about everything. Get ready for the return of Jesus.

PRAYER:

God, we are so thankful that you promised to come back. Help us not to worry about how it is all going to work out, but instead to pray about everything. We want to be ready for you!

ACTIVITY:

There are several ways that we can prepare ourselves for the return of Jesus. Call out the following suggestions while your children act out each one: be alert, pray, and study God's Word. Let others come up with their own suggestions for everyone to act out.

Did you know...

Ever since Jesus left the earth, people have been predicting the time of his return and not doing a very good job of it. The earliest known prediction was in the year 500 and was somehow based off the dimensions of Noah's Ark. One of the more recent predictions was that the return of Christ would correspond with a lunar eclipse scheduled to occur on September 28th, 2015. The eclipse came and went, but sadly, no sign of Jesus. We continue to believe that he will come back because he promised that he would. Be ready!

Two Are Better

Two people are better off than one, for they can help each other succeed. If one person falls, the other can reach out and help. But someone who falls alone is in real trouble. Likewise, two people lying close together can keep each other warm. But how can one be warm alone?

ECCLESIASTES 4:9-11 NLT

Have you ever been so cold that you have snuck into your parents' room to snuggle up in their warm bed? If no one was in that bed, it wouldn't be warm, would it?

God knows that people need each other; that's why he made so many of us and why he gives us family and friends. When you find people that you trust, remember to be kind and helpful to them, and make sure you ask them for help when you need it too. God created us to be in relationship with each other.

PRAYER:

Jesus, thank you for family and friends that we can be in relationship with. Help us to love each other by being honest, caring, helpful, and generous.

ACTIVITY:

Solitaire may be a good way to pass time but it's definitely not as fun as playing a game with friends and family. Take some time tonight to enjoy each other as a family while playing your favorite card game, for example, Go Fish, Crazy Eights, or Rummy.

Did you know...

Often portrayed as tricksters and con artists in popular folklore, wolves have a family life that is more loyal and pious than most human relationships. Normally, packs are made up of a male, female, and their offspring—making wolf packs like a family. The older offspring even help take care of their younger siblings. Sounds like wolves are better off together too.

Small Tasks, Big Meaning

Be kind and compassionate to one another, forgiving each other, just as in Christ God forgave you.

EPHESIANS 4:32 NIV

It can be fun to look for creative ways to serve other people. You might decide to pick a flower for your mother, or do the dishes without being asked. You might make a card for your dad, or help take care of someone when they are sick. Maybe you bring cookies to a neighbor who just had a baby. Or babysit someone's children so they can take a break.

The more you look for ways to serve, the more serving will become a part of who you are. The same thing happens with forgiveness. Every time we choose to forgive other people, it becomes easier to be a person who forgives.

PRAYER:

Jesus, help us to follow your example of serving, and help us to be quick to forgive others just as you forgive us.

ACTIVITY:

Have everyone pull out some blank paper and crayons and create a card to give to someone special. Be sure to include some kind words or draw a creative picture. Drop it in the mail or hand deliver it this week.

Jesus Helps

The Lord gives sight to the blind.
The Lord lifts up people who are in trouble.
The Lord loves those who do right.

PSALM 146:8 ICB

There were a lot of people that needed help when Jesus was on earth. People wanted to be healed from sickness and poor people needed food to survive. Jesus didn't forget about the people that were doing the right thing either. He knew that life could be hard for those who were following him.

Are there ways that we can be like Jesus? Can we find someone who is sick to pray for? Can we give something to someone who doesn't have much? There are a lot of people that need help in our world, and we have something very special to give them—the love of Jesus.

PRAYER:

Jesus, thank you for caring for everybody. Help us to see the needs in our world and to help where we can.

ACTIVITY:

Take a moment to think about the people at your church. Is there anyone sick who you could pray for? Do you know of any families who need practical help? Pray together as a family right now for those in need.

All Promises Kept

You believe in God through Christ. God raised Christ from death and gave him glory. So your faith and your hope are in God.

1 PETER 1:21 ICB

When we hope for things and never get them, it can be discouraging. When we do get something we hoped for, we often find the excitement wears off and we transfer our hope to something else. The reality is that anything we hope for in this life (that won't carry into eternity) won't keep us satisfied for very long.

We trust God and put our hope in him because what he promises us is true. When Jesus died on the cross and then rose again, he gave us hope that lasts forever. We know that every promise Jesus makes will come true.

PRAYER:

Holy God, we trust that you keep all your promises and we will always have hope because of you. Thank you that your hope lasts forever, and that we will never be disappointed when you give us what you have promised.

ACTIVITY:

Write the word HOPE vertically on this page. Then create an acrostic of God's promises by writing down words that start with each letter of the word hope. For example:
H = Help, O = Overcome, etc.

FRUIT SNACKS

SELF-CONTROL

Next to the situations below, write solutions
that demonstrate self-control.

1) Someone gets upset with you and pushes you.

2) You hear someone saying something about you
that is not true.

3) Someone ruins one of your very favorite things.

4) You get asked to do something that is someone else's job.

5) No one is listening to your idea.

Get a Glimpse

A single day in your courtyards is better
than a thousand anywhere else.
I would rather guard the door of the house of my God
than live in the tents of sinful people.

PSALM 84:10 NIRV

Imagine you are standing in the middle of two camps. On one side is a whole lot of little tents, only big enough to fit one or two people. On the other side is a beautiful huge castle, big enough to fit thousands. Where would you rather be? In the tents or at the door of the castle?

The writer of this verse said they would rather be at the door of God's great house than to be anywhere else. Don't you agree?

PRAYER:

Father, thank you that you are preparing a place for us to be with you forever. Help us to remember that being with you is more important than anything else in life.

ACTIVITY:

What do you think God's house looks like? Is it filled with gold and jewels? Are there many rooms? Draw a picture together of God's house. Be sure to include everyone's ideas to complete your masterpiece.

I Need Grace

God continues to give us more grace.
That's why Scripture says,
"God opposes those who are proud.
But he gives grace to those who are humble."

JAMES 4:6 ESV

If you were playing a game with friends and someone got bossy, telling everyone that you had to play by their rules, how would you feel? Would you want to do it their way? Now think of someone who kindly says that there might be a better way to play the game. You would probably listen.

Jesus wants to listen to people when they ask him with a good heart. If you try to tell him to do it your way, it doesn't show that you care about what is best. Being humble means listening to Jesus. And when you listen to him, he will give you grace.

PRAYER:

Jesus, thank you that you created us to need you.
Help us to know that you always have the best way in mind.
We want to show humility in how we live and in how we
ask you for things.

ACTIVITY:

God loves it when we pray with a humble heart. A big part of being humble is taking time to listen to God and not just talking to him. Pray as a family for God to give you a humble heart and ears to hear what he wants to tell you. Be sure to include a time of silence as you listen to God. If this is new to you, just try it for thirty seconds. Step out in faith and share with each other whatever you think God might have said during this time.

Did you know...

The Bible calls Moses a very humble man, more humble than any other man on earth. It's no wonder why God chose him to be the one to lead the Israelites out of captivity in Egypt.

More Mature

Christ will live in your hearts because you believe in him. And I pray that your love will have deep roots. I pray that it will have a strong foundation. May you have power together with all the Lord's holy people to understand Christ's love. May you know how wide and long and high and deep it is. And may you know his love, even though it can't be known completely. Then you will be filled with everything God has for you.

EPHESIANS 3:17-19 NIRV

The best trees to climb are the big ones because they have a lot of really strong branches. The biggest, strongest trees have roots that have grown so deep into the ground that they are almost as big as the tree itself!

Trusting the promises of God is kind of like a growing tree. As we get to know Jesus, our relationship with him grows stronger. As his Holy Spirit fills us, our love grows. As our love grows, our faith will grow, and in him we will do great things.

PRAYER:

Heavenly Father, help us to grow stronger and stronger in you by understanding more of your love. We want to be like strong trees with deep roots, and we know that we need to rely on you for that.

ACTIVITY:

Children often think that grownups are perfect and that they know everything, but learning from our mistakes is a powerful way that we can gain maturity in our lives. Share a story with your children of a time when you were young and made a mistake. What did you learn from this experience? How would you handle it differently in this stage of life? Let your example be an encouragement as they are on their own journey of maturity.

Did you know...

The average life span of a tree is about fifty years. However, some species like the Bristlecone Pine can live up to 5000 years! In fact, there is one tree in the White Mountains of California which has been named Methusaleh, and scientists believe it is 4,845 years old.

Holding On

You must hold on, so you can do what God wants and receive what he has promised.

Hebrews 10:36 icb

Do you like swings? How high can you go? What would happen if you let go of the ropes on the swing? You would fall! It's important that we hold on because this is what helps us go higher and stay safe.

The Bible says that we have to hold on to God like this. That means we keep following him all the days of our life. He has promised us a life in heaven, so don't ever let go of him.

PRAYER:

Lord, thank you for your promises. Thank you that you have shown us how to be dependable. We want to keep holding on to you through our whole lives. We can't wait to receive your reward of eternal life!

ACTIVITY:

When you open the fridge is there generally food inside? When it rains does your roof keep you dry? When you hurt yourself, are your parents there to help you feel better?

Discuss things that you depend on in your daily life. Parents do a pretty good job taking care of their kids, but they aren't perfect. However, God is our perfect example of dependability.

Koalas have special bacteria in their stomach that lets them live off an exclusive diet of highly poisonous eucalyptus leaves. Unfortunately, baby koalas aren't born with this nifty bacterium, so what's a momma to do? Well, she feeds her babies her non-toxic waste, of course! For the first six months of life, the baby koala is fully dependent on its mom while it lives in her pouch and builds its tolerance for eucalyptus leaves. Aren't you glad you are not a koala?

Ask

Don't worry about anything; instead, pray about everything.
Tell God what you need, and thank him for all he has done.
Then you will experience God's peace, which exceeds anything
we can understand. His peace will guard your hearts and
minds as you live in Christ Jesus.

PHILIPPIANS 4:6-7 NLT

The great thing about God is that he always knows what you need. When you need someone to talk to, he's there. When you need help, he's there. He is never going to leave you, and he is always delighted to hear from you.

We can pray to God even when we don't feel like we need anything. God wants to hear from us whether we're experiencing something good, bad, or something in between. When we talk to him, he gives our hearts peace because we know that he listens carefully, and he is big enough to take care of us.

PRAYER:

Lord, we give you our highs and lows today. Thank you for the joy that you have brought to us, and for your peace in the middle of trouble. We are so grateful that you listen to us when we talk. Help us to be better listeners too.

ACTIVITY:

Let's play the High and Low game! Going around the table, have everyone share one high and low point of their day. Take a moment to pray at the end, being sure to thank God for being with you in both the highs and lows of your day.

Say Yes

*The yes to all of God's promises is in Christ,
and through Christ we say yes to the glory of God.*

2 Corinthians 1:20 NCV

We hear a lot of no's in our life. No, you can't go out with your friends. No, you can't have another piece of cake. No, you can't bring your new toy to school. No, you aren't getting a promotion at work. No, we can't afford a new car. It's pretty great when we get to hear yes, isn't it?

God made a lot of good promises. He said that we would be forgiven. He said that we would be part of his family. He said that we would have eternal life. The best thing is he made all of these promises come true by sending Jesus to us. All you need to do is to say yes to Jesus, and all of God's promises will come true in your life.

PRAYER:

God, we say yes, right now, to your promises for our life. We say yes to your forgiveness, yes to being a part of your family, and yes to eternal life!

ACTIVITY:

Scripture tells us that testimonies are powerful and life giving! Share with your kids tonight about when you first said yes to Jesus. It's helpful to also talk about what it looks like to say yes to Jesus on a daily basis.

Various cultures have different ways of making promises. When people testify in a court of law in America, they put their right hand on a Bible and swear to tell the truth. In the ancient Jewish world, they didn't really have Bibles; instead, they would place their hand under each other's thigh when making a promise. Yes, you read that right. Whether they were selling a house or buying a cow, they might have grabbed each other's leg to seal the deal. And we thought shaking hands was odd.

FOR WHAT WE HAVE RECEIVED, WE ARE TRULY THANKFUL...

Make a list of things your family is thankful for.
Remember to look at this list frequently so you can
live with an attitude of gratitude!

No Greater Love

This is how we know what real love is: Jesus gave his life for us. So we should give our lives for our brothers.

1 John 3:16 icb

There isn't a better example of love than Jesus Christ. He gave up his entire life for love. He left the beautiful heavens and came down to earth so we could spend forever with him. He did what was best for us!

While many of us won't actually have to die for another person, there are plenty of ways to show our love for others. The best way to show love is to think about what is best for the other person just like Jesus did for us.

PRAYER:

Jesus, thank you for giving up your life in heaven and coming to earth to rescue us from sin. Help us to love others the way you love us, by preferring them over ourselves.

ACTIVITY:

There are many ways we can prefer one another in our daily lives. Stepping in and helping someone with their chores and responsibilities is an easy way to show that you love them. Could you offer to clear your brother or sister's dishes tonight? Pick a job that someone else usually does in your family and offer to take care of it this week.

Best Treasures

Since you became alive again, so to speak, when Christ arose
from the dead, now set your sights on the rich treasures and
joys of heaven where he sits beside God in the place of honor
and power. Let heaven fill your thoughts; don't spend your
time worrying about things down here.

COLOSSIANS 3:1-2 TLB

Everyone around us seems to care about clothes and movies and things. Did we get the latest phone, computer, game console, car, or tv? It is hard not to think about material possessions a lot.

The best treasures are in heaven. That's what God wants us to think about more than things on earth. Let's be careful what we watch, look at, and think about. We would do much better to keep our minds on God and his Word.

PRAYER:

Father, please help us turn away from the things of
this world, and set our hearts on heaven. We want to reap
eternal rewards that come from obeying and serving you
while we are here on earth.

ACTIVITY:

It's easy in our society to get overwhelmed with stuff! Most of us probably have a hard time keeping our room clean because we have too many toys. Have your kids go through their things and set aside one or two items to be dropped off at a donation center. Being selfless and thinking about others is one way we can store up treasures in heaven.

Did you know...

After its inception in 1955, the Guinness Book of World Records quickly went on to become a household name. There are so many people eager for recognition, in 2006 over 100,000 people participated in ten different countries in an attempt to break world records and get their name in the book of fame.

Be Your Best

He knows how we were made.
He remembers that we are dust.

PSALM 103:14 ICB

Can you jump higher than a building? Can you walk through walls? Can you walk on water? Of course not! Our bodies weren't made to do things like that. There are plenty of amazing things about how our bodies were created and how they work, but we weren't made to be invincible.

When God made our bodies, he didn't make a mistake. We were created to live a great life, but God didn't want us to be superheroes. He wants us to be the best we can be, and leave the rest to him. Being our best is enough!

PRAYER:

Father, you designed us exactly how you wanted us each to be. Help us to love the bodies that you have given us and to keep them healthy. Teach us to do our best and to leave the rest to you. Thank you for accepting us just as we are.

ACTIVITY:

Ask everyone to write down two things they are really good at, and one thing that they are not so good at. Go around the table and have everyone read their lists out loud. Remind your kids that God doesn't expect us to be perfect, but he does want us to do the best we can with what we have.

Did you know...

Michael Phelps starting swimming at the age of seven simply because his mom wanted him to know how to swim. By the age of ten, Phelps held the national record for 100-meter butterfly. He competed in his first Olympic games in Sydney 2000. He went to the 2004 Olympics in Athens and won his first gold medal—actually six of them. Phelps broke another record at the Beijing Olympics in 2008: he won eight gold medals. He won six more medals in 2012, and another six in 2016. His total medal count is 28, which makes him the most decorated athlete in Olympic history!

Older and Wiser

First, I tell you to pray for all people. Ask God for the things people need, and be thankful to him. You should pray for kings and for all who have authority. Pray for the leaders so that we can have quiet and peaceful lives—lives full of worship and respect for God.

1 TIMOTHY 2:1-2 NLT

Who is older than you? Your parents, your teachers, your babysitter, your boss. When you are young, it seems like most people are older than you are. Think about how much older some people are. Is it ten years? Twenty years? Thirty years, or even more?

Older people know more because they have lived a lot longer. If you trust the older people around you, make sure you listen to what they say. Try to understand that they know better than you do. This is what respect is all about.

PRAYER:

Father, thank you for the older people in our lives who care about us. Help us to always respect them, and to pay attention when they speak to us. We want to show them that they are valued and important.

ACTIVITY:

One way we can show respect to others is by showing gratitude. Make a thank you card for a grandparent, a teacher, or someone else who is older than you are. Write a few words to let them know how much you appreciate their impact on your life.

Try Not to Fight

Be sure that no one pays back wrong for wrong. But always try to do what is good for each other and for all people.

1 Thessalonians 5:15 icb

When someone shoves you, do you shove back? If they say something mean, are you mean too? No matter who starts a fight, everyone who is involved will reap some kind of consequence.

It's hard not to fight back, but that's just what God wants us to do. He doesn't want the problem to get worse, so he asks us to do good for each other—even for people who are not very nice. We will always feel better when we choose to do the right thing.

PRAYER:

Father God, fill us with your goodness. Help us not to fight back when people upset us. We want to show patience and forgiveness toward others. Help us to bring your peace to troubled situations.

ACTIVITY:

It can be hard to do the right thing in the heat of the moment. Tonight, let's practice ways to respond to difficult situations. Role play scenarios when someone says or does something mean to you. Let your kids suggest both the right and wrong ways to respond.

Stand Your Ground

Remain strong in the faith. Don't let anything move you. Always give yourselves completely to the work of the Lord. Because you belong to the Lord, you know that your work is not worthless.

1 CORINTHIANS 15:58 NIRV

Do your parents give you jobs around the house? They might ask you to take the trash outside, or to help clear the dishes, or to set the table. There might be some gross jobs like cleaning the toilets. Parents have hard jobs too.

What if none of the household jobs were done? We would have a home full of trash, dishes with old food stuck on them, and dirty toilets! If you don't think that's a big deal, you should know that all those extra germs can build up and make people sick. God wants us to be responsible. Everybody has work to do. When we choose to take care of our responsibilities, God rewards us.

PRAYER:

God, help us to be joyful about the jobs that we have to do. We want to be responsible and give ourselves completely to your work. Thank you that you see everything we do, and you will reward us for it one day.